A WINE LOVERS GUIDE

To Red Grape Varieties

By

Greg Adams ▢

Foreword

This book is the first in a series that focuses on providing appealing and useful information on popular red wine grape varieties. This book is meant to serve as an introduction on the topic and hopefully will prove to be an enjoyable read and worth having to hand.

Table of contents

Introduction

This book is an introductory manual for people who love wine. Nowadays, there is a lot of information at your disposal on the Internet which can be sometime be misleading or confusing. Therefore, I believe that there is a need for a handbook like this one; which summarises a lot of data without the need to read a full sized textbook. The reader-friendly format this book supports will allow you to check the information with just a quick glance. Furthermore, this short book is just the first of a series which will cover a lot of wine related subjects including other grape varieties as well as wine growing regions.

As you already know, one of the main uses for grapes is to produce wine. This beverage has been the theme of odes and poems since the time of Ancient Greek. They even had a god that supported the consumption of wine, Bacchus (also the name of a grape variety). But why is there so much agitation around this drink? Maybe it is because of the uncontested taste of wine. Or maybe it is because of the aroma. Whatever the reason, this beverage has definitely been popular for millennia and remains fashionable and always growing in popularity.

If food pairing or marrying is of interest to you then this book will also be useful as it covers the basics of matching wine with food.

Experience is the best when it comes to food matching. Have you tried wine and cheese? This combination is very popular because the acidity and base match perfectly. However, although most wines match well with cheese, some choices are better than others. This is not an exact science though, as the appreciation may vary from one person to another.

Personally, I prefer white wine with cheese in summer because it seems more refreshing. Red wines are mainly recommended with meat but can also be served with starters that contain cheese. You see, the possibilities are endless regarding wine-pairing.

Most of the time, we choose a meal and then a wine that matches. Not the other way around. However, if you really enjoy one type of wine you should go for it. One advantage of learning how to pair wines with your meals is that you will avoid uncomfortable experiences in restaurants. In fact, this knowledge will present you a world of possibilities to your taste and smell. Who hasn't followed the recommendations of someone else regarding wines choices just to find the pairing not to your taste, or to be suppressed with the good match. By learning these skills you won't need to rely on others.

If you like soft flavours, such as goat's cheese, rosé Champagne is the way to go. There are other interesting choices such as Sauvignon Blanc, Pinot Noir or Merlot. On the other hand, stronger wines will pair well with stronger cheeses.⍰

Why read this book?

There are quite a few reasons to include this handbook to your reading list. As you have already noticed, wine is a suitable beverage to enhance the taste of your meals. However, there are so many types of wine which often courses confusion to newcomers in wine-pairing decisions. Do you prefer red wine or white wine? Reading the following pages will allow you to arrive to a conclusion on how to accompany your meals with an adequate wine.

Moreover, if you can't make up your mind yet, you will be able to try a few suggestions that I provide. This book contains just some of the most popular red grape varieties, there are hundreds more and you will learn more about rare grape varieties in another book in this series. I believe that separating the content in to some smaller handbooks will improve the readability of the content. Furthermore, great things come in small packages, right?

How to read this book?

In order to facilitate the reading experience, the chapters are mostly independent in this book. The format is quite straightforward so that you can move from one part to another with a glance within the chapters.

The lists and bulleted points make the reading a breeze. You can take a look at the points of interest without wasting any precious time. In addition, I have separated the content in manageable paragraphs to make it even easier for you to go through the content.

The Red Varieties

The wines which only contain one type of grape are called varietals. For instance, a Cabernet Sauvignon wine is named after that grape variety. In these wines, the variety of grape is fully responsible for the flavour of the wine. Wines that are made of more than one grape variety are known as blends, these includes wines such as Rioja, which is made of several grapes blended together. We provide useful information for newcomers to the wine world who are willing to learn the relevant info without being saturated by the overwhelming flow of data online.

My goal is to introduce you to the basics of this dense and fascinating topic. Now that you know what you should expect from this light handbook, we shall delay the journey no more. Let's get immerged in the red grape varieties!

Cabernet Sauvignon

History

The origin of the variety Cabernet Sauvignon has remained unclear for quite a while. In fact, some myths and conjectures were created to explain the origins of this grape. "Sauvignon" probably comes from the French word sauvage, which means wild. The wild variety of grape that is indigenous to France is Vitis vinifera. So, most likely the name referred to this variety in the first place.

However, the ancient origins of this grape were not confirmed. Some people believed it was the authentic Biturica used by the ancient Romans, which was described by Pliny the Elder. During the 18th century, this variety of grape was commonly named as Petite Vidure or Bidure, which derived from the word Biturica, because of these suppositions about its origins.

Moreover, some people found a relation with the Carménère variety because it was named Grand Vidure for a while. There was also another theory, which pointed out that the Cabernet Sauvignon grape vine originated in the Rioja region of Spain.

Afterwards, the name Cabernet Sauvignon started to kick in and became prevalent. Some people point out that it was also called Petite Vidure but that is not 100% certain. What is sure is that the grape was very popular in the Bordeaux planting zone about two centuries ago, more specifically in the Médoc region. From that moment, this variety has remained very popular in the region.

Tasting

Cabernet Sauvignon has a wide range of flavours due to the large geographical distribution of the plantations that grow this variety. As it can come from different locations, the flavour varies. This variety is a full-body red wine that contains dark fruit flavours; it tastes like black pepper or even like bell pepper. In order to understand how the flavour can differ, we will compare two different regions that grow this variety of grape.

The 100% original Cabernet Sauvignon wine from Europe is sort of unusual because winemakers in the Old World prefer to blend some varieties together. However, this kind of wine tastes mostly like herbal or floral flavours, such as graphite, violets and tobacco. These flavours surpass the fruit scents that this pure blending transmits.

On the other side of the Atlantic, we have the mostly fruitier savours that are originated in the New World. You can taste black cherries, Liquorice and black pepper and even a hint of Vanilla. This wine has more alcohol, less acidity and a slightly lower amount of tannins. As you can see, the same variety of grape can provide us with a really different taste.

Location

This variety of grape can grow in very different regions of the world. The following list summarizes some of the most important locations where you can find Cabernet Sauvignon and the main differences that they provide to the taste of the wine.

Bordeaux. This is probably the most famous region that produces this variety and exports to the rest of the world. This wine has bold tannins, black plum, tobacco leaf and a dash of oak spice savour. It is a strong choice that pairs perfectly with many meals.

Napa Valley. This valley is also very relevant in wine production but is not as famous as the Bordeaux region. The wine from this location has full body, providing a strong flavour, firm tannins, a birth black cherry scent that cannot be underestimated, pepper and vanilla flavours.

Washington. Another wine producing region that should not be overlooked when you search for tasty wines. The tannins of this wine are big and velvety, the flavour contains a juicy blackberry flavour. Moreover, you should expect the blackcurrant and mocha influence in the mix.

Coonawarra. This is a rather different wine which contains supple tannins; terra rossa soil traces of minerals and an uncontested combination of black fruit, eucalyptus and mint leaf in the mix which makes this wine stand out from the rest.

South Africa. A large winemaking region that export to the rest of the world. The wine from this location contains ripe tannins, rich fruit flavour, mint leaf, herbs and oak traces. The combination provides a soft savour that is quite tasty.

Chile. The wine from this region contains supple tannins, blackcurrant, eucalyptus and dashes of oak.

Growth Info

Cabernet Sauvignon is able to grow in a wide range of climates zones all over the world. This grape can create a varietal wine or serve as a component in a blend. Among the major grape varieties, this is the last vine to bud and ripen. For instance, it takes about one or two weeks more than Merlot and Pinot Noir varieties. The climate of the growing season influences strongly on how early the grapes will be harvested. Cabernet Sauvignon is commonly harvested earlier in zones where there is a risk to have the vines affected by the cold season, such as the Bordeaux region. On the other side, in regions that are exposed to warmth or over-ripening, the wine is likely to develop stewed blackcurrants flavours.

Food matches

Due to the strong flavour of this wine, there is the chance to overwhelm delicate meals. Furthermore, the high tannin content and the oak elements in the wine influence the wine matching possibilities depending on the regional cuisine. The younger the wine is, the stronger those elements are. The wine mellows as it ages, though. Therefore, more food pairings become possible due to the flavour strength variation.

Most of the time, the weight of the wine, i.e. the alcohol level and body, should be considered when pairing the wine with meals. In this step, the heaviness of the food happens to be the most relevant consideration. High alcohol levels and spicy foods are not recommended. Moreover, milder spices, like black pepper, match with this wine because they lower the perception of tannins. The classic choice is Cabernet Sauvignon with steak au poivre and pepper – Definitely worth a try!

Blending

Arguably the most popular blend is the one from Bordeaux, which contains Cabernet Sauvignon, Merlot and Cabernet franc. Sometimes, the bland can also have Malbec, Petit Verdot and even Carménère. In the United States, the Meritage designation is the one which also combines similar varieties. However, Cabernet Sauvignon can also be blended with Shiraz, Tempranillo and Sangiovese.

The most important factor to determine the blending is the moment, either before, during or after the fermentation. Most wine producers prefer to ferment and age each variety on their own. Then, they blend the wine just before bottling.

Carménère

History

Carménère is one of the most ancient varieties of grape in the Old World namely Europe. Some people consider that this variety is a long-established duplicate of Cabernet Sauvignon, However, this variety was probably named after the original Vidure, which is a local Bordeaux name that refers to a Cabernet Sauvignon clone. This is due to the fact that people used to believe that there was one original grape variety that originated all the Bordeaux grapes that grow nowadays in the region.

In this context, Carménère was also thought to be the ancient Biturica, which the Romans used to produce wine centuries ago. Biturica was the old name that the Bordeaux region had back in Roman times. Recent studies point out that the variety of grape was originated in Iberia, in the Spanish and Portuguese wine growing areas. Pliny the Elder described a popular blending in his time, which contained Sangiovese called Predicato di Biturica in Tuscany.

The Carménère grape is thought now to be indigenous to the Médoc region of Bordeaux in France. Sadly, it is nearly impossible to find Carménère wines in France nowadays because of the Phylloxera plague that took place in 1867. Most of the vineyards in Europe were damaged in that year. The scope of the plague was so deep that the Carménère variety was thought to be extinct. As a consequence, planting this variety was abandoned after this catastrophe.

Tasting

The Carménère grape creates a strong red wine that has intense flavour and an inky violet colour. The aroma that will stand out in this wine from the first moment is tobacco and you will also notice tar, leather and dark fruit. The flavour echoes in the nose because of its strength. You will notice the cherry and blackberry traces in the taste. There are also some more flavours, such as blueberry, plum, pepper and vanilla. As you can see, tasting this wine is quite an experience for the senses.

Location

Fortunately, this variety was not extinct two centuries ago during the large plague that devastated Europe. Carménère grape has become more popular in the past few years. More importantly, this variety is also appealing outside France at this moment. For instance, in Chile, wine makers have preserved this grape variety due to the large similarity that it shares with the Merlot grape. As a consequence, we can find this grape in quite a few blends without much effort due to the huge effort of the growers.

During the 19th century, cuttings of Carménère were imported to Chile by growers from Bordeaux due to reasons such as the confusion with Merlot vines in the region. Moreover, the difficulty of this variety to be grown in France also influenced in this decision cosidering that the weather conditions in Chile were more favourable. This was really fortunate because the plantings in the valleys around Santiago made the preservation of this grape possible.

In 1990, the Ca' del Bosco Winery purchased Cabernet Franc vines from a French nursery but they were mistaken. In fact, those vines belonged to the Carménère variety, which grows in the northeast part of Italy. Since 2007, this variety was approved to have the Italian DOC wines from Veneto, Friuli-Venezia Giulia and Sardinia. This variety of grape is also grown in the Eastern Washington region, in Walla Walla Valley as well as in California, United States.

You can find this variety in other parts of USA, such as California's Lake County. Louis Pierre Pradier is a French research scientist and viticulturist who is responsible for preserving this Carménère variety. On the other side of the globe, in Australia, Dr Richard Smart exported cuttings of this grape in the 90s. The first nursery was planted in 2002 and nowadays the Carménère wine is used in Angels' Share blend. This variety has also reached New Zealand.

Growth Info

The Carménère variety requires excellent conditions to grow successfully. This is the main reason why the popularity decayed in France. However, the efforts by some wine lovers have made it possible to preserve the grape. This plant often presents problems ripening once it experiences cool spring weather conditions. Therefore, the warmer climates favour the growth of this variety. That is why Chile, Australia and some regions in the USA are a good match for this special grape.

Food matches

Carménères flavour is gentler and a bit softer than the Cabernet Sauvignon variety. This is a medium-body wine that is compatible with lighter meals. This grape is mostly used in blends but wineries also produce bottles of pure varietal Carménère. Optimal ripeness creates a cherry-like, fruity flavour which contains spicy traces. The wine has a deep crimson colour that is quite appealing. This grape is a great choice to produce wine that you can pair with steaks, pasta and meat-based sauces. Grilled food and spicy meals are also a suitable match for this wine.

Blending

The Carménère variety requires a long growing season in mild to warm climates. Over-watering the vines help to enhance the herbaceous and green pepper flavours of this wine. This grape variety is produced in most wineries to be used in blending in order to accentuate some characteristics of the wine. This grape combines with Cabernet Sauvignon, Cabernet franc and Merlot most of the time. The varietal wine of Carménère is also possible but less frequent.

Grenache

History

The Grenache grape variety is named Garnacha in Spain and was probably originated in the region of Aragon, located in the northern most part of Spain. Plantings spread from the original region to that of Catalonia. Later, lands under the Crown of Aragon, such as Sardinia or Roussillon in southern France, also had this variety.

The wine produced with this grape was commonly named as Tinto Aragonés, red of Aragon. In Sardinia, this variety was known as Cannonau. By the time people had claimed that Sardinia was the place this variety originated, the grape could be found at both sides of the Pyrenees. However, despite the Spanish origins, Garnacha was not planted in the Rioja region – the most important wine-producing spot in the country - until the century after the Phylloxera epidemic struck Europe. This grape arrived in Australia back in the 18th century and was one of the first grapes to be planted there.

Nowadays, it is the second most popular red wine grape variety only surpassed by Shiraz some decades ago. California wine growers have also grown this variety since the 19th century. The hot San Joaquin Valley is the best spot for this grape, which is a common a component in pale, sweet jug wines blends.

Tasting

The uncontested candied fruit flavour and cinnamon scents in this wine make it stand out from the rest of its kind. This wine has a medium to full weight in the mouth. However, it has a lighter colour, characteristic of this variety and is, in fact, semi-translucent.

Grenache often contains strong smells which vary depending on the region it was planted. There is a notable range of flavours in this wine, from orange rinds to ruby-red grapefruit flavours. In the Old World plantings, such as Côtes du Rhône or Sardinia, the wine may also have herbal notes of dried oregano and tobacco.

Location

The Grenache variety is one of the most common red wine grape varieties in the world. France and Spain are the two largest wine regions that produce this variety. In the past century, the Tempranillo, Cabernet Sauvignon and Merlot varieties were favoured in Spain. Thus, the terrain for the Granache variety decreased. As a consequence, France is the current world's largest source of Grenache, where this grape is produced behind Merlot and Carignan in quantity.

Most French wines that contain the Grenache variety are blends but there are also varietal wines produced in fewer amounts. Wines from the Rhone and southern French regions are mostly linked to this grape. According to History, the influence of Burgundian wine merchants can be tracked down to the use of Garneche two to three centuries ago, when winemakers needed to add body and alcohol to their lighter wines. As a consequence, Grenache became increasingly popular.

Garnacha is probably the grape's original name, which was given in Spain. Among the clones of this variety, we can find the dark coloured Garnacha Tinta (or simply, Tinto) which is also the most common. The Garnacha Peluda or Hairy Grenache which has a hairy texture on the underside of the vine's leaves is another grape that can be found in Aragón.

The latter produces wines with lower amount of alcohol and higher acidity. It also contains savoury notes more as the wine ages. This grape is considered of low quality and it mostly used for blending. However, Priorat in Catalonia lead to a reconsideration of this status during the past century.

Nowadays, this variety of grape is the third most popular in Spain just behind Tempranillo and Bobal.

As a matter of fact, the Denominación de Origen (DO) wines in Aragon, Catalonia and Navarra and other certifications serve to validate the high quality of this grape. Aragon is thought to be the most probable origin of this grape and currently concentrates the largest surface of Grenache plantings. The DO of Calatayud, whose production is 91% of Grenache, is defined as old vines because they are 35 years old as a minimum. In Rioja, the grape is planted in the warmer areas named Rioja Baja, and is frequently blended with Tempranillo. In Navarra, which is close to Aragon, the grape is harvested earlier in order to benefit from the fruitier flavour.

This variety can also be found in Italy; it grows in Sicily, Umbria and Calabria.

Growth Info

This grape variety grows better in the arid conditions of its indigenous country, Spain. This is why Grenache occupies more vineyard acres than other varieties in the country. This grape is also an essential component of the Chateauneuf-du-Pape in the southern Rhone region of France. It is also required to produce the Tavel and Lirac, which are among the most famous French rosé wines.

Food matches

Grenache has some spicy notes that make it perfect with spicy and herby meals. Roasted meats, vegetables and several eastern foods are suitable candidates to be accompanied by this wine. This wine is great with almost any spicy food, try with curried goat!

Blending

This wines main purpose is to add body and sweet fruitiness to the mix. However, the grape tends to oxidize easily and loses colour, which makes it difficult to handle in the wine production. In order to compensate for the low tannins and phenol compounds, harsh pressing and hot fermentation are preferred by some winemakers.

Surprisingly, you can also find this variety in Cyprus, where it serves to produces a wine called Kykko: a blend of Grenache and Carignan. On the other side of the globe, in Australia, Grenache and Shiraz are united to elaborate high-quality red table wine.

In fact, the high levels of sugars in the wine in combination with the lack of harsh tannin favour Grenache in producing fortified wines. The vin doux naturels (VDN) of the Roussillon region is a good example of these properties. There are also interesting products from Australia that are known as the port-style wines, which contain 15% to16% of alcohol. Both of these types of wines have such longevity they can even be consumed up to 30 years after their bottling without the best features disappearing.

Malbec

History

The Malbec variety is a purple grape that usually shows an inky dark colour. This grape serves to elaborate strong wines and is, in fact, one of the six varieties that are combined in the blend of red Bordeaux. Nowadays, most of the plantations of this variety are located in Cahors, which is in South West France. This grape is known as Auxerrois or Côt Noir in Cahors, Malbec in Bordeaux and Pressac in other regions. Back in 1956, frost killed nearly 75% of the crop. After the catastrophe, the variety became immediately less popular.

However, Malbec was replanted in Cahors after the frost and remained popular in that region until present day. It is often mixed with Merlot and Tannat in order to produce dark, full-bodied wines. Recently, Malbec varietal wines have been produced, as well. Regarding the name of this variety, there is a story that points out a Hungarian peasant as being responsible for spreading the grape variety in France at first. The French viticulturist Pierre Galet, however, states that Côt was the variety's original name.

He also points out that this grape is indigenous to northern Burgundy. The Malbec variety has been confused with Malbec argenté, which is in fact a variety of the south-western French grape Abouriou. The former has also been labelled Auxerrois Blanc by mistake on some occasions. The Malbec grape has a thin skin and needs more sun and heat than Cabernet Sauvignon or Merlot to mature completely. This variety ripens mid-season and presents a very deep colour. It produces ample tannins and its particular plum-like flavour is quite characteristic.

In the new world this grape is planted mainly in the Mendoza region of Argentina although there are some other important plantings, such as Buenos Aires and La Rioja. Nowadays, the Malbec grape is an important asset in the South American wine-making sector as it has become an internationally highly rated product. The Mendoza region is a well-known zone for viticulture plantings due to the favourable climate conditions.

Tasting

This grape produces rich wines with dark colour and juicy flavour. Malbec is used to produce really inky red or violet wines which have a lot of intensity. Thus, this grape is useful in blends, like those which contain Merlot and Cabernet Sauvignon. The result is the red French Bordeaux blend. It produces ample tannins and its particular plum-like flavour is quite characteristic to the grape.

This wine is well known for a couple of strong reasons, firstly, dark fruit flavours and smoky elements are the introduction card for every Malbec wine. In the colder regions, this wine transmits more of a black cherry taste. Secondly, the warmer regions provide this wine with a blackberry taste. The grape from Argentina has blackberry, plum and black cherry elements whereas the French wine is just the opposite. In other words, you should expect tar currant, black plum and a bitter flavour in this European wine.

Location

The Malbec variety can be frequently found in several regions of the world. Each region produces a slightly different grape whose properties are worth comparing. A comparative study conducted by the Catena Institute of Wine and University of California, focused on analysing the phenol composition of Malbec wines. As a result of this research, the conclusion was that there are undeniable differences between the wines produced in California, in the USA, and Mendoza, in Argentina.

In the Cahors region, the Malbec grape is clearly the dominant red variety. Moreover, the Appellation Controlée regulations in this zone demand a minimum content of 70% of this grape to be legally accepted. French agricultural engineer Michel Pouget exported this variety to Argentina back in 1868, where is widely planted nowadays. In Argentina, this grape produces a softer wine with less tannic content than in France.

Whereas this grape is losing popularity in Cahors and other French regions, it has become the national variety of Argentina. Although the variety was introduced to the region in the 19th century, it wasn't until the late 20th century it became popular. The fruity flavour and the velvety texture of this Argentinean wine are its strongest points.

Growth Info

Regarding the most evident features, the Malbec grape has a thin skin and clearly needs more sun and heat than Cabernet Sauvignon or Merlot to mature completely. This variety ripens mid-season and differs from other grapes because it presents a very deep colour. Unfortunately, Malbec is really susceptible to various grape diseases and viticulture hazards, such as frost, colure, and others. On the bright side, the development of new clones and the refinement of techniques related to vineyard management have reduced these issues.

This variety grows well in most soil types but it does better in the limestone-based soils, such as in Cahors. In this region, it seems to produce the darkest colours and the highest tannic content. In fact, the clones of Malbec found in France and in Argentina are different. In the latter, the Argentine Malbec is the grape variety that is planted and it tends to have smaller berries than its European counterpart. Mendoza is the leading wine-producing region in Argentina, the vast majority of growers favour this grape variety.

Food matches

The pairing depends on the kind of wine that you are aiming to use. For instance, young fruity Malbec pairs well with meat-strong meals, such as beef, meatballs, burgers, burritos, etc. On the other hand, full-bodied Malbec pairs well with the heaviest meals that contain meat, such as steaks, roast beef, lamb, etc. Cahors or Côt are suitable choices to pair with lamb, duck, sausages and so forth.

Now, what dishes are perfect matches for this wine? One strong choice is the skirt steak with Chimichurri sauce, which is an Argentinean meal traditionally named as gaucho steak. Do you like lamb? In that case, braised lamb shanks with four bean and chorizo stew is a great pick in the cold season. Not to mention that barbecue and grilled chorizo pair very well with Malbec wines.

In addition to the meat pairings, you could also consider some spices and herbs in the pairing decision. Those herbs that have earthy and smoky flavours are the best pick, such as rosemary, garlic. This is a wine worth considering in any tasty upcoming meal.

Blending

This variety of grape is often blended in order to produce the wines of Bordeaux. In this blend, Merlot, Cabernet Sauvignon and Petit Verdot are the common grapes. In Argentina, this grape is also mixed with an Italian variety, Bonarda. Although this grape works well in blended wines and brings a lot of flavour, it is also widely used on its own and in some markets is the most popular grape variety sold.

⁇

Merlot

History

The Merlot grape variety is a dark blue grape which can become a component in blends and also varietal wines. The name most likely comes from the French word merle, which refers to a blackbird and is likely linked with the colour of this grape. This grape was first mentioned back in the 18th century and the current name appears later, this could be due to the interaction between the bird and the vine. Apparently, blackbirds like eating this grape.

The most important varieties in France are the Cabernet Sauvignon, Cabernet Franc, Malbec, Petit Verdot and, of course, the Merlot. In fact, this is one of the most relevant assets of Bordeaux wine. Furthermore, Merlot has a really popular demand in many wine markets due to this, Merlot has recently become one of the world's most planted grape varieties.

After a couple of unfortunate events, such as a severe frost in 1956, this variety was banished between 1970 to 1975 by the authorities in the Bordeaux region. Later on, the good press provided the headlines that supported the consumption of wine because of its healthy properties. In addition to this, the name of the wine was easy to pronounce, which also contributed to its spread accross the USA. These circumstantial facts and the uncontested quality of the wine have made it possible for Merlot to spread all over the world.

Tasting

The Merlot variety produces wines that are considered to be between the Pinot Noir and the Syrah. In other words, you should expect red fruits and soft tannins in the mix. In addition to these characteristics, Merlot is known for having a soft finish. As a matter of fact, some important differences are worth noting between the grape grown in cold and warm climates. The variety allows winemakers to create the beverage that they desire to fulfil their aims.

In cold regions, Merlot has a higher presence of tannins and earthy flavours. Sometimes, these kinds of wines are confused with Cabernet Sauvignon due to such features. On the other side, we find a fruitier flavour in the wine that is produces in warm climates. In these liquors, the tannin content is more reduced. In this regard, some winemakers opt for having the wines treated in oak barrels so that it acquires more structure after a couple of years.

Location

This variety of grape can be found all over the world as it is currently one of the most widely spread grape varieties. France still produces most of the Merlot grown in the whole world. Italy also favours this variety and there are plantings of this grape in many other regions, such as Romania, Australia, Canada, etc.

In southern France, there is a large amount of this variety being produced yearly under the designation of Vin de Pays wine. In the Bordeaux blend, the Merlot is expected to add body and softness to the combination of grapes. In Italy, most of the Merlot grape is blended with Cabernet Sauvignon and Cabernet Franc. An important percentage of the production is also blended with Sangiovese, especially in Tuscany. This is a tasty wine which is popular in the southern region of Europe, close to the Mediterranean Sea.

Growth Info

This grape can be severely damaged in the winter and is also susceptible to disease. The variety can grow in cold or warm climates but the different ripening times should be considered if you want to have a high quality wine. Also, soil problems can affect the growth, such as a low amount of zinc, salinity and other issues. As a consequence, some winemakers have favoured other varieties that are more resilient, especially in the regions with harsher climate conditions.

The popularity of the Merlot variety is due to the appeal that the New World wines have nowadays, which favours late harvesting. These kinds of wines have an inky purple colour and are full in body. The intense plum and the blackberry traces are characteristic of this wine. On the other hand, if winemakers prefer the Bordeaux wine style, they need to harvest the Merlot sooner to assure that the levels of acidity are as required. This procedure elaborates medium-bodied wines which have a moderate content in alcohol and red fruit favours. As you can see, both options are adequate for different customer profiles.

Food matches

Merlot has such diversity that it is compatible with a wide range of meals. As we have already noted, Cabernet varieties pair well with Merlots. Grilled and charred meats are a good match for this wine. however, the softer and fruitier Merlots share most food-pairing attributes with Pinot noir. In this case, these wines match perfectly with salmon, mushrooms and greens.

On the other hand, light-bodied Merlots match better with shellfish, such as prawns or scallops. Try to avoid strong and blue-veined cheeses because they could overwhelm the flavours of this wine. Spicy foods, however, are likely to enhance the perception of alcohol in Merlot coursing the wine to taste bitter. This wine is a perfect match for some tasty meats that are popular in most meals.

Blending

This variety stands out for some good features, such as its softness, fleshiness, and the early ripening that is has. Due to this, the Merlot is a popular grape that often appears in combination with the later-ripening Cabernet Sauvignon. The Merlot is softer in tannins whereas the Cabernet Sauvignon has a slightly higher amount of tannin and a fuller body. Therefore, the combination of both serves to obtain a wine without too much tannin.

When winemakers produce a varietal wine, the result is soft wines with plum favours. Merlot matures faster than Cabernet Sauvignon; there are also wines that age in bottles and can be aged for decades. As the wine remains in oak, it acquires notes of caramel, vanilla and coffee. The characteristics of the wines vary considerably depending on the blend and the treatment that the wine receives once bottled.

Pinotage

History

The Pinotage variety is a grape that was created in South Africa in 1925. Abraham Izak Perold who was the first Professor of Viticulture at Stellenbosch University was the first planter of the vines. This expert was trying to combine the best features of some grapes in order to create a better variety. Thus, the robust Hermitage and the Pinot noir were combined in the production of this variety. The result was a grape that produces great wine but is somehow delicate to climate conditions.

However, the grape survived almost by chance. In 1927, Charlie Niehaus saved some plants before the university garden was cleaned up due to overgrowth. There plants were moved to Elsenburg Agricultural College. Some years later in 1941 the first wines were bottled. Soon after, this wine started to become increasingly popular and acquired great fame. One outstanding feature of the Pinotage variety is that it is able to mature for up to 25 years. Therefore, this is the grape which produces the most refined wines of South Africa today.

Tasting

Pinotage has a somewhat misleading name because it sounds similar to Pinot Noir. Some people could and do assume that they have a similar taste but this is not true. Actually, this South African grape has a similar appeal and taste to that of Shiraz. However, the Pinotage variety is somehow related to Pinot Noir. The information held on this variety from the last century has provoked some misconceptions though. During the past couple of decades, Pinotage has received some bad press and gained somewhat of a bad reputation meaning sales have declined.

The bold barbecue-friendly wine that the Pinotage produces is very appealing. The main objective of Perold, the creator of this variety, was to obtain a tasty wine as delicious as Pinot Noir with better growing characteristics, like those of Cinsaut. While tasting this wine, you will find purple and black fruits traces. You will also notice delicious red fruit flavours, such as raspberry, red liquorice or red bell pepper.

The best quality wines that are produced with Pinotage provide flavours more than just fruit notes. The flavours that are present in this wine are dried leaves and sweet pipe tobacco. There are bold tannins that transmit a sweet note similar to flavoured smoke. This grape tends to have a high pH level, which means a low acidity. In order to increase the acidity of the wines, during the fermentation process the wine producers add this acid content in the wine structure. The Pinotage grows better in hot climates, such as California, Australia and Argentina, where the acid content is slightly higher.

Location

South Africa is the largest zone where Pinotage is planted but this is not the only region where winemakers favour this variety. You can also find this grape in Brazil, Canada, Israel, USA and Zimbabwe. In the US, plantings are located in Arizona, California, Michigan, Oregon and Virginia. Also, German winemakers have recently started to use this grape. In South Africa, winemaking traditions allow a wide range of plantations for this variety.

The Cape blends contain this grape in an important percentage in order to produce a full range of wine styles. You can either make easy-drinking wines or barrel-aged wines. The fortified port style is preferred in red sparkling wine. However, this grape is highly dependent on the skill and style of the winemakers. The grape has deep coloured, fruity notes that can be found in young and old wines. In New Zealand, Zimbabwe, Germany, USA, Israel and Brazil this variety becomes progressively more popular.

Growth Info

The Pinotage vines have been proven to be disease-resistant, as they were expected to be in the first place. This is a rather hardy and productive variety. However, it presents some issues regarding viral diseases. The Pinotage variety clearly prefers sunny locations but not too hot. In fact, too much heat can produce an unpleasant flavour in the wine if it takes place at the end of the growing season. However, the fermentation process is also delicate provided that high temperatures can boost the acetone-like flavours to spread in the final product.

Due to the exigent conditions that the production process requires, this wine acquired a bad reputation 30 years ago. The naturally high-yielding Pinotage plantations ended up producing several insipid wines in the past century. Therefore, popularity reached a minimum during the 1980s. Luckily, winemakers reconsidered the use of this grape nearly a decade after these unfortunate events once the restrictions were lifted regarding this variety. Nowadays, the style and the skill in the production process influence the final result. Most of the time, the grape is blended with Cabernet Sauvignon and Shiraz in order to make high-quality wines.

The success of this variety outside South Africa is not as spread. For instance, there are some plantations in New Zealand North Island, in the Hawke's Bay and Auckland. This plant is also found in California and Israel.

Food matches

In order to find the best matches for this wine, you should consider the pairings that do well with Pinot Noir and Cinsault, the grapes which created this variety in the first place. Smoked duck and pork are really appealing choices to consider with this wine. Some Mediterranean meals match perfectly with this wine, such as French bistro dishes. Peppers and aubergines are also suitable ingredients to combine in the food you wish to pair with the Pinotage.

In South African cuisine, we find plenty of examples for the combinations. From marinated lamb to Cape Malay and even Cajun-spiced fish are adequate candidates for these pairings. If you prefer veggie food, you should consider aubergines, grilled mushrooms and dark greens to taste the most amazing combination of flavours.

Blending

The proportion of Pinotage in the Cape blend has a minimum value of 30% and the maximum quantity is 70%. For instance, the Simonsig Frans Malan Reserve contains 60% Pinotage with Cabernet and Merlot. A wine that has a lower percentage of Pinotage, close to 36%, is the Beyerskloof Synergy 2001 Stellenbosch, which also has 25% Cabernet and 39% Merlot.

⁉

Pinot Noir

History

Pinot Noir is a red wine grape variety that is used for varietal wine and blends. This variety is also used to produce champagne. The name stands for the French words for pine and black. The reason for this name is the fact that this kind of grape is tightly clustered just like "pine-like" bunches grape. This fruit can grow in several regions worldwide but prefers the cooler regions, such as the Burgundy region in France.

Other important wine-producing regions that grow Pinot Noir are Willamette Valley in Oregon, the Carneros, Central Coast and Russian River, American growing Areas of California, the Walker Bay wine region of South Africa, Tasmania and Yarra Valley in Australia and the Central Otago, Martinborough and Marlborough wine regions of New Zealand.

According to recent data, Pinot is a very ancient variety whose origins remain unclear. About 900 years ago, Columella describes a grape similar to this current variety in his book De re rustica. That grape was located in the Burgundy region. Before the phylloxera plague, there were wild vines that grew north Belgium, though. Therefore, it is possible that current Pinot Noir is a direct domestication of these wild vines, Vitis sylvestris.

Tasting

This is a variety which has a quite characteristic taste. You can expect a fruity flavour, like that of cranberries, cherries and raspberries. You should note vanilla, liquorice, mushroom, wet leaves, tobacco and even caramel aromas. As you can see, this wine is packed with a wide variety of scents. Also, its medium-to-low tannin content transforms it into a soft experience. This wine usually has medium-to-high acidity and it can age from 2 to 18 years in barrels (mostly oak). The Pinot Noir grape is one of the varieties that has a really unique taste and serves to classify other wines according to the proximity to this varietal wine.

Location

The Pinot Noir grape can grow in many places around the world. In Australia, this variety is very successful planted in quite a few regions, such as the Southern Highlands, the Yarra Valley, Adelaide Hills, and others. The cooler zones favour the growth of this kind of grape. You can also find Pinot Noir in Austria, where it is often aged in French barriques (barrels). The main wine-producing regions for Pinot Noir in Austria are Burgenland and Lower Austria.

In the Niagara Peninsula of Canada, there are Pinot Noir vineyards. This variety is now the second most planted in the UK, where it is used to produce English sparkling wine. Obviously, there are many regions in France where this grape can be found. On one side, Burgundy is known for having aged wines. On the other hand, wines produced in regions, like Champagne or Alsace, are lighter in style.

In Germany, expensive wines which are rarely exported are made from this variety. This variety is also popular in Italy. Although it was widely planted in Moldova, the phylloxera plague severely damaged the vineyards. This variety is also popular in some other countries, such as Slovenia, Spain, Switzerland and the USA.

Growth Info

This grape has one of the earliest harvesting dates in relation to other varieties. This kind of grape is preferred in regions where climate does not allow grapes to get to complete maturity provided that this is a short-season grape. Therefore, marginal locations which have harsher climate conditions favour this kind of grape vastly. In addition, the temperatures are cooler when the plant blooms so that the characteristics of the grape depend on this fact.

Food matches

This is a very flexible wine which is great if you have just ordered meat and fish dishes. Thus, Pinot Noir is a no brainer pick if you just happen to be unsure on what to try next time. It's an excellent choice most of the time so you will be making a smart decision. Duck and mushrooms pair with most Pinot Noir wines. The same happens with salmon and tuna, although the marriage varies depending on the type of wine and how the fish is prepared.

Light fresh pinots like the cheap red burgundy pair well with charcuterie, ham and cold meats. Sweetly fruited pinots match well with spicy dishes, such as crispy duck, pork, etc. These kinds of wine are mostly produced in Chile, New Zealand and California. Silky elegant pinots are perfect accompanied with roast chicken. Lamb and grilled steaks should be served with full-bodied pinots and the older wines, such as the older vintages of Burgundy are a good choice if your meal has pheasant or any other game meat in it.

Blending

This grape is one of the main components of Champagne –
Chardonnay and Pinot Meunier are the other two varieties
that take part in this blend. Thus, Pinot Noir is often seen as
a component in sparkling wines and have an important
touch of its delicious and delecate features. On the other
hand, this grape is rarely used in still wines. For instance, a
touch of Syrah can help to produce a heavy red wine with
this variety.

Shiraz

History

This is probably one of the most ancient grape varieties as Shiraz (also known as Syrah) has a really long documented history. It is not clear if this grape is indigenous to the Rhône region in the south-eastern area of France but it has got a lot of references to this region. About two decades ago, a study conducted in France concluded that Syrah was the offspring of the grape varieties Dureza (father) and Mondeuse Blanche (mother). This study was based on DNA typing techniques and extensive grape reference material from the area.

On one side, Dureza is a dark-skinned grape indigenous to the Ardèche region in France. Although this grape has been banished from the vineyards, it has been preserved in Montpellier. On the other side, Mondeuse Blanche is a white grape variety from the Savoy region. This grape is still planted in very small amounts in the regions vineyards to this day.

Neither of them has achieved Syrah's fame or popularity in any moment of History. Moreover, there is no evidence that supports the possibility of these varieties being cultivated in other distant regions. According to these facts, Shiraz most likely originated in the northern area of Rhône. The name of this variety became popular in Australia as a substitute for the previous name, Hermitage, which was not that catchy in some countries. There are legends which suggest that this grape comes from the Shiraz, in Iran, which is famous for the Shirazi wine.

However, the origin of the name in Australia dates from mid-19th century and had no relation with the city in Iran provided that it was first spelled as Scyras. Later on, this name changed to its current form: Shiraz. Most likely, the influence of English in a French name was the cause of the switch in spelling. Nowadays, the wine is commonly labelled as Syrah of Shiraz.

Tasting

This wine has a strong taste which contains fruits like blackberry and blueberry. Olive, vanilla and mint notes should be noticeable in the favour. Aging this wine in oak barrels is a common choice most of the time. This grape produces a wine with a medium level of tannins. The same should be expected regarding the acidity. The common aging abilities of this wine go from 5 years to 9 years. However, in exceptional cases can range from 12 years to 25 years.

Location

Recently, this grape has been taken many places around the world. The warmer regions are the best places to grow this variety. During the last 20 years, vineyards of this variety have increased considerably. In Australia, the variety is popular and there are many regions it is now grown. In the Rhone Valley, France, this grape remains a strong pick among wine producers. The same applies to the USA wine-producing regions. On the other hand, in Spain and Italy this grape is often seen as a blending variety. However, Portugal produces both varietal and blends using Syrah.

In Italy, the regions where this grape mostly grows are the Tuscany, Lazio and Apulia. The wines that are produced in these regions are highly valued in the international market due to the amazing quality of the beverage. As expected, France is one of the most important wine-producing countries for this grape. The differences in the soils and the terrains produce a wide range of wines which are a dream come true for any wine lover. This grape adds structure to Grenache blends in order to elaborate wines such as the famous Côtes-du-Rhône. The arguably but likely region that originated this grape remains as the most relevant in its production. In Switzerland, the variety produces concentrated red wine. On the other side of the globe, Australia has large vineyards full of this grape. This variety is a component for SGM, which is a blend that comprises Shiraz, Grenache and Mourvèdre.

Shiraz is also planted in South Africa, where the vineyards have expanded a lot in the past few decades. In the USA, the grape is commonly refered to by the French name,

Syrah. However, when wine makers use a New World style to elaborate the wines, they prefer to label them as Shiraz. Most of the growers in Washington and Naches Heights use this variety.

You can also find wines from Chile and Argentina that are made using this grape.

Growth Info

This variety is mostly planted in warmer regions because cold temperatures can seriously affect the flavours. Cooler temperatures create a spicier taste in the wine. On the other hand, the warmer conditions favour the plum taste and produce a less spicy and slightly heavier wine.

Food matches

There are quite a few meals that can be accompanied by Shiraz. Grilled or Roast beef are two of the dishes that should be served with this wine. However, barbecued foods are also an adequate choice with this wine. The same applies for big beefy stews and even kangaroo – were you in Australia! Strong cheeses can be enjoyed with this delicious wine as well.

Blending

The blends vary from one region to another as Shiraz can be planted in many regions of the work. For instance, the Bosworth Puritan Shiraz 2011 and the Bobar Syrah 2009 (from Yarra Valley) are two Australian blends. The first is an early wine that most people may like whereas the second is a tricky wine to pair due to the fact the weather conditions can provide you with a really different sensation on the palate. Cabernet Sauvignon and Shiraz are a common blend that was first used in mid-20th century. You can also find Grenache and Viognier in the same blend with Shiraz. Most of these wines pair well with dishes that have high meat content.

Final Words

As you have seen throughout this book, there are several major grape varieties and all varieties do not have the same flavours, different regions create completely different wines.

Now that you are familiar with some of the basic knowledge regarding red wines from all over the world, it should make it slightly easier you to decide which ones to try first and which ones you are more likely to enjoy.

There are many other red grape varieties and some of these will be covered in other parts of this series.

If you enjoyed this book then please leave a review, and check out the other books in this series.

As a thank you for reading this book, I have included a link below to download a completely free and exclusive eBook.

As a thank you for downloading this book, I would like to offer you one of my books free of charge.

To get my Top 10 Wines To Buy In 2016 book just follow the link below.

https://gregadams.gr8.com

Thank you again!